SPECTACULAR SOLAR STORMS

Scott Wilken

An Imprint of Abdo Publishing
abdobooks.com

abdobooks.com

Published by Abdo Publishing, a division of ABDO, PO Box 398166, Minneapolis, Minnesota 55439.

Printed in the United States of America, North Mankato, Minnesota
052025
092025

Design: Elena Klinkner, Mighty Media, Inc.
Production: Mighty Media, Inc.
Editor: Ruthie Van Oosbree
Cover Photograph: satori/Adobe Stock
Interior Photographs: Alexey Seafarer/Shutterstock, p. 15; artiom.photo/Adobe Stock, p. 28 (paper towels); Denis Belitsky/Shutterstock, pp. 26–27; Francesco de Mura/Wikimedia Commons, pp. 16–17; Frederic Edwin Church/Wikimedia Commons, p. 20; Graphic Resources/Adobe Stock, p. 28 (black paper); Jana Buryskova/Shutterstock, pp. 22–23; Michael Fair/Adobe Stock, p. 28 (crayon); Mighty Media, Inc., p. 29; NASA, pp. 5, 25; NASA, ESA, and J. Nichols (University of Leicester), p. 12; NASA/ESA/SOHO, pp. 8–9; NASA/SDO, pp. 7, 19 (sunspots); Richard Carrington/Wikimedia Commons, p. 19 (Carrington Event illustration); Serghei V/Adobe Stock, p. 28 (chalk); Simon's passion 4 Travel/Shutterstock, pp. 10–11; Ulia Koltyrina/Adobe Stock, p. 7; Uncle-Ice/Adobe Stock, p. 28 (water glass)
Design Elements: Mighty Media, Inc.

Library of Congress Control Number: 2024949048

Publisher's Cataloging-in-Publication Data
Names: Wilken, Scott, author.
Title: Spectacular solar storms / by Scott Wilken
Description: Minneapolis, Minnesota : Abdo Publishing, 2026 | Series: Weather wonders | Includes online resources and index.
Identifiers: ISBN 9781098296407 (lib. bdg.) | ISBN 9798384917830 (ebook)
Subjects: LCSH: Storms--Juvenile literature. | Sun--Juvenile literature. | Solar activity--Juvenile literature. | Space--Juvenile literature.
Classification: DDC 551.6--dc23

Contents

Super Storms 4
Solar Flares 6
Coronal Mass Ejections 8
Atmospheric Effects 10
Ancient Impressions. 14
The Carrington Event. 18
Storm Surge 22
Wondrous Weather. 26
Draw an Aurora!. 28
Glossary 30
Online Resources. 31
Index 32

Super Storms

The sun constantly sends **energy** into space. This energy affects everything around the sun for millions of miles. It makes life on Earth possible by warming the planet. Sometimes the sun releases an extra burst of energy. This is known as a solar storm.

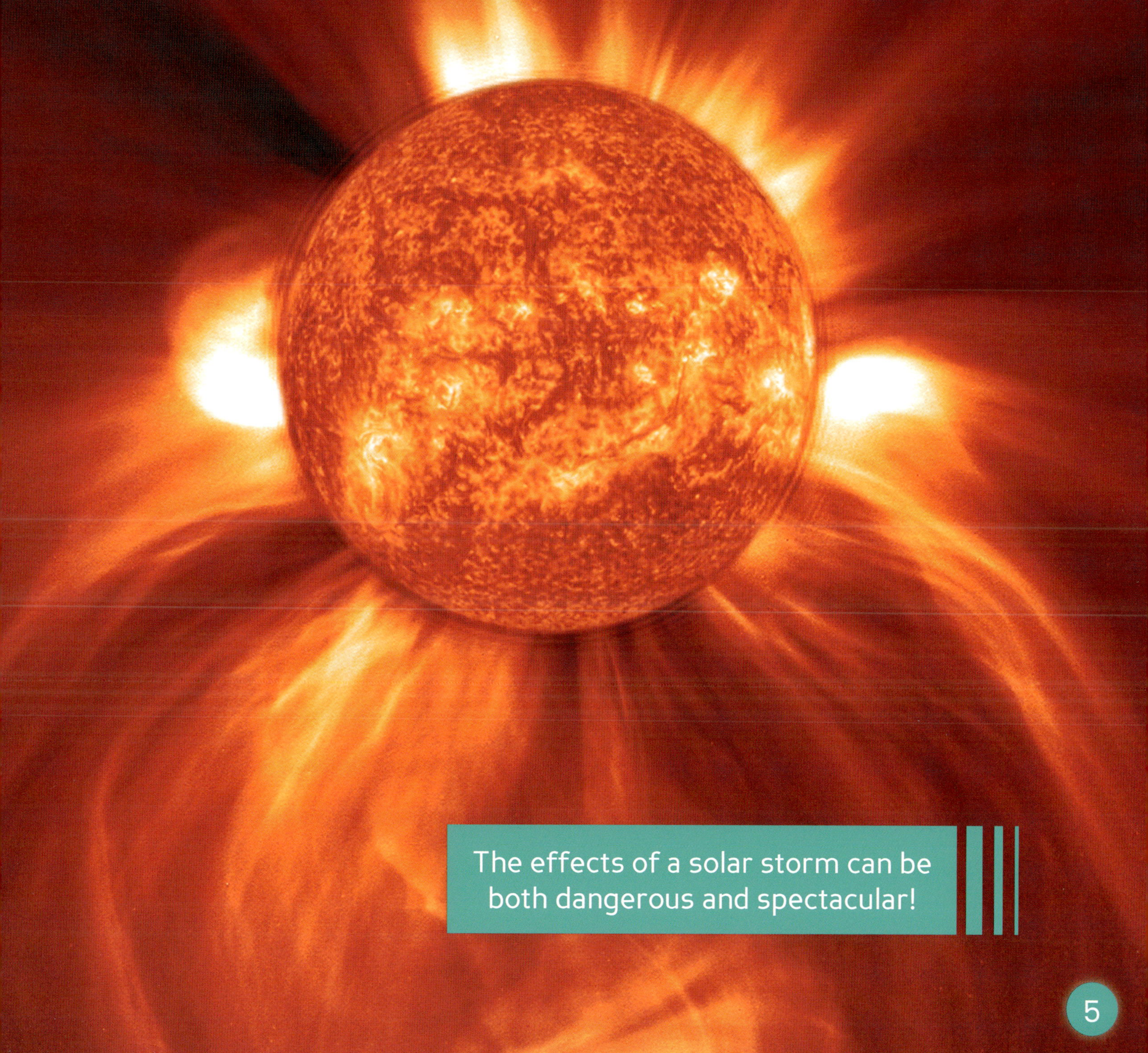

The effects of a solar storm can be both dangerous and spectacular!

Solar Flares

A solar flare is a type of solar storm. It is an explosion on the surface of the sun. The **energy** from a solar flare can cause problems. It can affect radio **communications** and **satellites** around the Earth.

The energy from a solar flare can reach Earth in less than ten minutes!

Coronal Mass Ejections

Another type of solar storm is a coronal mass ejection (CME). A CME is an explosion of **energy** and **plasma** from the sun. When CMEs reach Earth, they can be harmful. They can damage **satellites**, hurt **astronauts**, and even shut down power on Earth.

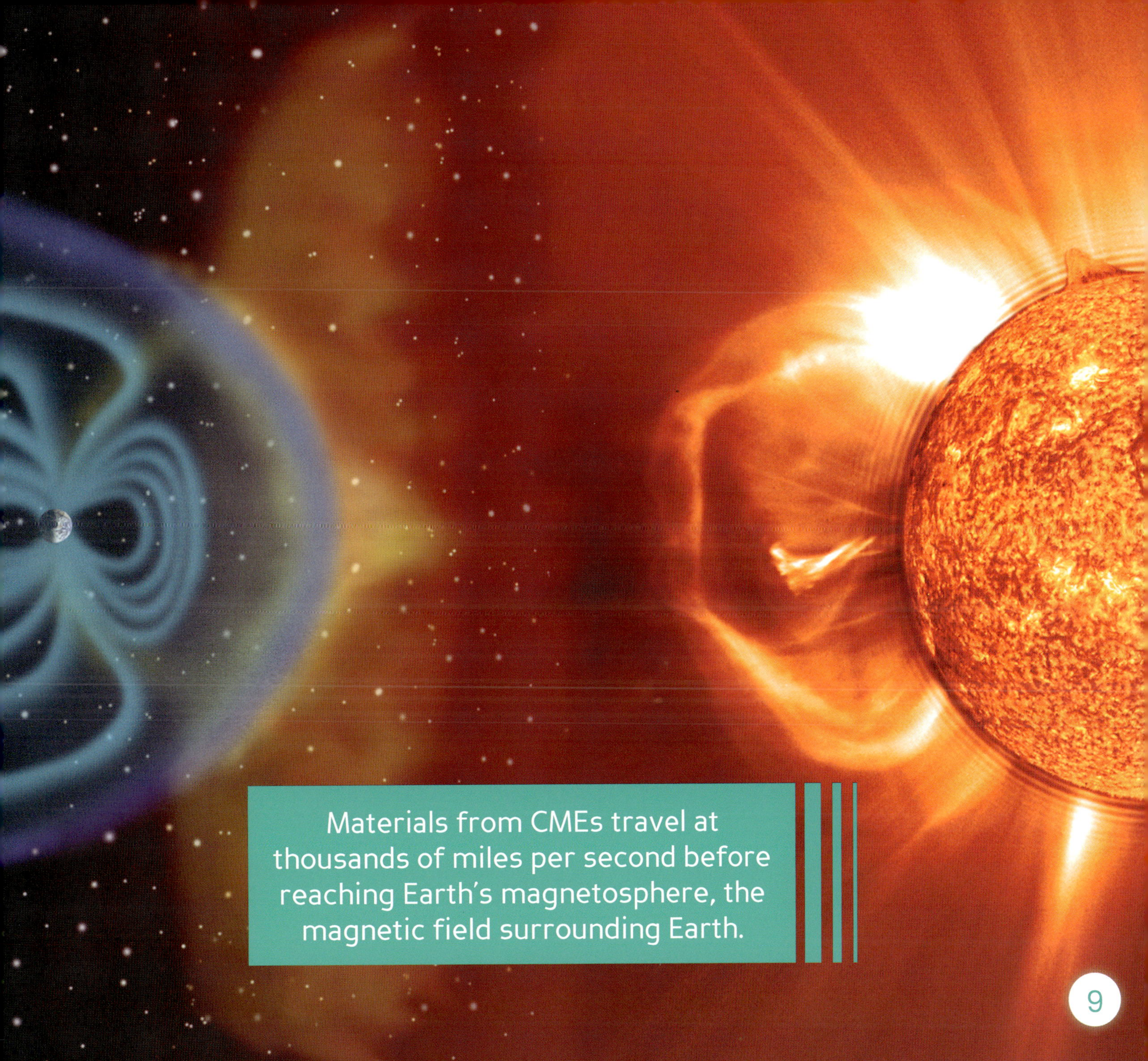

Materials from CMEs travel at thousands of miles per second before reaching Earth's magnetosphere, the magnetic field surrounding Earth.

Atmospheric Effects

When solar storms reach Earth, they can create light shows in the sky. The **energy** in a solar flare or CME contains small **particles**. These particles **interact** with the gases in Earth's **atmosphere**. This creates wavy streaks of colorful light called auroras.

Green, red, blue, and purple are common aurora colors.

Scientists have seen auroras on Saturn and Jupiter (*pictured*).

The **particles** in a solar storm are **attracted** to Earth's north and south poles. Auroras are easiest to see in those areas. An aurora in the northern **hemisphere** is called the aurora borealis or northern lights. An aurora in the southern **hemisphere** is called the aurora australis or southern lights.

Ancient Impressions

Ancient peoples didn't know what caused auroras. They had different **myths** explaining them. Some stories said the aurora borealis was associated with fire. Menominee Indians believed it was the torches of giant fishermen. Some Algonquin tribes believed it was from a fire lit by their creator.

In Finland, it was said that Arctic foxes created the aurora borealis. The myth claimed they ran so fast their tails started fires as they brushed against snow or mountains.

Other stories said the aurora borealis was associated with life after death. The Sami people of northern Scandinavia believed auroras were the souls of the dead. In North America, some Indigenous peoples believed it contained the souls of their dead ancestors.

Auroras are named after Aurora (*draped in orange*), the Roman goddess of dawn.

The Carrington Event

On September 1, 1859, British scientist Richard Carrington was studying the sun's surface. He observed two bursts of light on the sun. They lasted about five minutes. This became known as the Carrington Event. It was the first scientifically recorded solar storm.

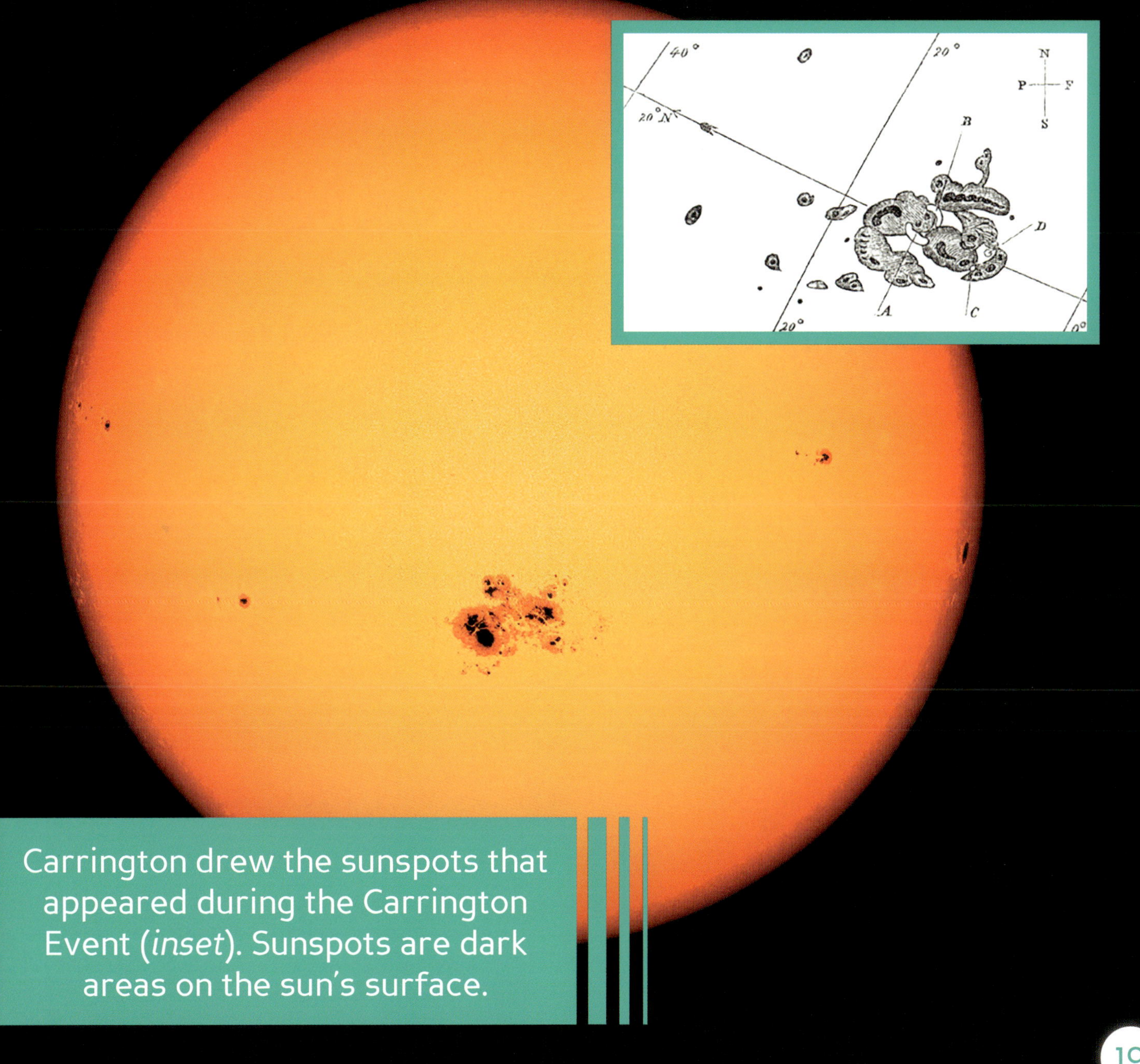

Carrington drew the sunspots that appeared during the Carrington Event (*inset*). Sunspots are dark areas on the sun's surface.

American artist Frederic Edwin Church painted *Aurora Borealis* in 1865. People have wondered if he was inspired by the Carrington Event.

The Carrington Event affected **telegraph communications**. It also caused a huge aurora borealis. These effects began the day after Carrington observed the bursts of light. So, he thought the bursts of light might be the cause.

Storm Surge

In May 2024, one of the biggest solar storms in history reached Earth. The **energy** from multiple strong solar flares and CMEs sped toward the planet. The CMEs all hit Earth's **atmosphere** at about the same time.

The May 2024 solar storms created bright auroras. They could be seen almost all around the world.

The solar flares in May 2024 were detected right away. Scientists were able to warn **satellite** operators and power companies. They had time to prepare for the coming solar storm. So, satellites and power grids avoided damage.

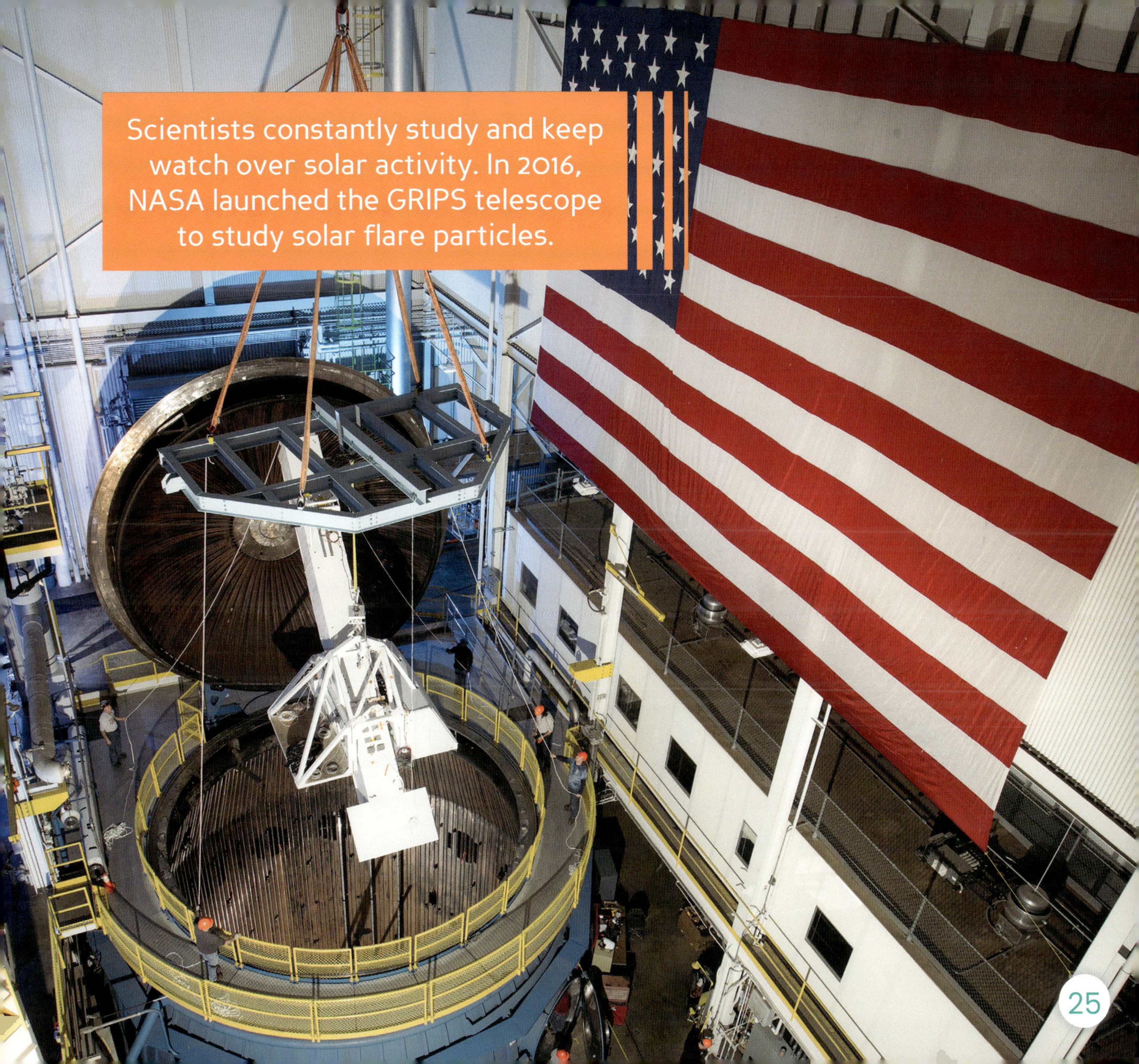

Scientists constantly study and keep watch over solar activity. In 2016, NASA launched the GRIPS telescope to study solar flare particles.

Wondrous Weather

Solar storms can cause many problems on Earth. But scientists continue studying them to protect people from their effects. Meanwhile, we can enjoy the **spectacular** light shows they create!

The aurora borealis is always occurring. But it is only visible in certain places and at certain times.

Draw an Aurora!

What You Need

- black paper
- white crayon
- colored sidewalk chalk
- paper towels
- water

What You Do

1. Use white crayon to draw mountains and stars on the black paper.
2. Draw a few thick, wavy lines in sidewalk chalk above the mountains. Press down firmly as you draw.
3. Wipe upward along each line a few times with a damp paper towel.

Glossary

astronaut—a person who is trained for space travel.

atmosphere (AT-muhs-feer)—the layer of gases that surrounds a space object.

attract—to pull closer.

communication (kuh-MYOO-nuh-KAY-shun)—giving and receiving information, such as knowledge or news.

energy (EH-nuhr-jee)—usable power. Heat is one form of energy.

interact—to have an effect on each other.

myth (MITH)—a traditional story that explains history or natural events.

particle—a very small piece of matter, such as an atom or molecule.

plasma—a substance that is similar to a gas but can carry electricity.

satellite—a spacecraft in orbit around a heavenly body.

spectacular—beautiful and amazing to look at.

telegraph (TELL-uh-graff)—a machine used to send messages across wires.

Online Resources

To learn more about solar storms, please visit **abdobooklinks.com** or scan this QR code. These links are routinely monitored and updated to provide the most current information available.

Index

Algonquin, 14
ancient peoples, 14, 16
astronauts, 8
atmosphere, 10, 22
auroras, 10, 11, 12, 13, 14, 15, 16, 17, 20, 21, 23, 27, 28

Carrington Event, 18, 19, 20, 21
communications, 6, 21
coronal mass ejections (CMEs), 8, 9, 10, 22

Draw an Aurora! project, 28, 29

Earth, 4, 6, 7, 8, 9, 10, 13, 22, 26
energy, 4, 6, 7, 8, 10, 22

Indigenous peoples, 14, 16

May 2024 solar storms, 22, 23, 24
Menominee, 14
myths, 14, 15, 16

plasma, 8
power, 8, 24

Sami, 16
satellites, 6, 8, 24
scientists, 12, 18, 24, 25, 26
sky, 10
solar flares, 6, 7, 10, 22, 24, 25
sun, 4, 6, 8, 18, 19

telegraphs, 21